DATE DUE

	204		
211			

GREAT MOMENTS IN
WOMEN'S SPORTS

by Michael Teitelbaum

WORLD ALMANAC® LIBRARY

Please visit our web site at: www.worldalmaniclibrary.com
For a free color catalog describing World Almanac® Library's
list of high-quality books and multimedia programs,
call 1-800-848-2928 (USA) or 1-800-387-3178 (Canada).
World Almanac® Library's fax: (414) 332-3567.

Library of Congress Cataloging-in-Publication Data

Teitelbaum, Michael.
    Great moments in women's sports / by Michael Teitelbaum — North American ed.
       p. cm. — (Great moments in sports)
    Summary: Recounts ten high points in the history of women's athletic competitions, including
Babe Zaharias's performance at the 1930 Olympics, the All-American Girls Professional Baseball League,
and the final game in the 1999 Women's World Cup.
    Includes bibliographical references and index.
    ISBN 0-8368-5349-0 (lib. bdg.)
    ISBN 0-8368-5363-6 (softcover)
    1. Sports for women—History—Juvenile literature. 2. Athletes—Biography—Juvenile literature.
3. Women athletes—Biography—Juvenile literature. [1. Sports for women—History.] I. Title.
II. Great moments in sports (Milwaukee, Wis.)
GV709.T45   2002
796'.082—dc21   2002016860

This North American edition first published in 2002 by
World Almanac® Library
330 West Olive Street, Suite 100
Milwaukee, WI 53212 USA

This U.S. edition © 2002 by World Almanac® Library.

An Editorial Directions book
Editor: Lucia Raatma
Photo researcher: Image Select International Ltd.
Copy editor: Melissa McDaniel
Proofreader: Sarah De Capua
Indexer: Tim Griffin
Art direction, design, and page production: The Design Lab
World Almanac® Library editorial direction: Mark J. Sachner
World Almanac® Library art direction: Tammy Gruenewald
World Almanac® Library production: Susan Ashley and Jessica L. Yanke

Photographs ©: Getty Images, cover; Corbis, 3, 4; Getty Images, 5, 6; Popperfoto, 7, 9 top;
Getty Images, 9, bottom; Corbis, 10, 11, 13 left, 13 right, 14, 15 top, 15 bottom, 16;
Corbis/Sygma Archive, 17; Popperfoto, 18; Getty Images, 19, 20 top; Popperfoto, 20
bottom; Associated Press, 22; Getty Images, 23, 24, 25, 26, 27, 28, 29, 30, 31, 33 left, 33
right; Getty Images, 34, 35; Reuters/Popperfoto, 36; Corbis, 37, Getty Images, 38, 39, 40;
AFP, 41; Getty Images, 42, 43, 44, 45; Corbis, 46 top left; Getty, 46 bottom left, right.

Printed in the United States of America

1 2 3 4 5 6 7 8 9 06 05 04 03 02

Opposite: *Sophie Kurys of the Racine Belles—*
one of the many teams created in the 1940s
as part of the All-American Girls Professional
Baseball League—hook slides during a July
1947 game against the South Bend Blue Sox.

Contents

Introduction

Perhaps the most important moment in the history of women's sports didn't take place on any field, court, rink, pool, or track. In 1972, the U.S. Congress passed Title IX of the Education Amendments, ending discrimination against girls and women in federally funded education and sports programs.

Before this, there were only a few sports programs in which girls and women could compete. Women's college programs lacked the money received by men's. Only a few years after Title IX, participation by girls and women in high school and college sports more than tripled. Title IX's gift of equal funding opened the door to millions of girls and put an end to the idea that sports were only for boys.

As far back as 776 B.C., when the first Olympic Games were held in Greece, women were not only banned from competing but were actually put to death if they were caught watching the games! Undaunted, the Greek women formed their own, unofficial games.

At the 1960 Summer Games, Wilma Rudolph made Olympic history by winning three gold medals in track-and-field events, a mark that inspired women in all sports to achieve excellence.

That spirit was also in evidence in 1896, the year of the first modern Olympics. Denied the chance to compete in the marathon that year, two women ran the 42-kilometer course on their own, one a month before and the other the day after the official event.

This desire to excel, improve, and challenge oneself is as human as the need to breathe. Throughout history, women have felt this desire as strongly as men and have challenged themselves to pursue excellence in the world of sports. Because of Title IX, today's generation (and future generations) of girls and young women simply take for granted that playing sports is a part of growing up—for everyone. That fact alone will lead to many great moments in women's sports in the coming years. This book contains the stories of some of those women who—through their determination, talent, and hard work—have left their mark on the world and inspired others to strive for greatness.

Choosing ten great moments to feature in this collection was a challenge in itself, and

The 1999 U.S. World Cup team captured the imagination of soccer fans and served as role models for female athletes in a variety of sports.

there are obviously many great moments that are not included here. Many might argue that some great achievements have been left out, but such arguments are part of what makes being a sports fan fun. Even though choosing only ten great moments was tough, the athletes who made the final cut represent the best of the best.

Whether it's Babe Didrikson Zaharias dominating any sport she tried, Wilma Rudolph overcoming a disabling childhood illness to attain Olympic gold, Martina Navratilova winning nine Wimbledon tournaments and setting a new standard for women's tennis, or Joan Benoit Samuelson proving that women could indeed run a marathon, all the women featured in this book displayed courage, commitment, and a passion for excellence to go with their incredible talent.

THE GREATEST EVER

Babe Didrikson Zaharias at the 1932 Olympics

Mildred "Babe" Didrikson Zaharias earned her nickname growing up in Port Arthur, Texas, in the 1920s. As a young girl, she could kick a football farther, throw a baseball harder, and hit a baseball better than any of the boys in her neighborhood. The boys called her "Babe" after their idol, slugger Babe Ruth. The name stuck.

Even today, few people will argue the fact that Babe Didrikson was the greatest female athlete of all time. Grantland Rice, the leading sportswriter of the 1930s, called her the most perfect example of "complete mental and physical coordination the world of sport has ever

At the 1932 Games in Los Angeles, Babe Didrikson set an Olympic record in the javelin throw.

known." Her astonishing ability became apparent in elementary and junior high school, where she excelled in basketball, but it came into full blossom at Beaumont High School in Port Arthur, where she played on—and dominated—every women's team: volleyball, basketball, baseball, tennis, swimming, and golf.

Amazing Athlete

After high school, with very limited athletic opportunities for women at colleges, Babe went to work for a company called Employers Casualty. This company in Dallas, Texas, fielded a team sanctioned by the Amateur Athletic Union (AAU), the governing body for all amateur teams in the United States. From 1930 to 1932, Babe led her company's basketball team—the Golden Cyclones—to two finals and one national championship.

During her time at Employers Casualty, Babe also discovered track and field, competing in AAU meets in shot put, discus, javelin, high jump, long jump, hurdles, and the baseball throw. She set new U.S. records in the javelin throw and the baseball throw.

Babe became an instant celebrity—and she loved every minute of it. Brimming with confidence to the point of being boastful, she relished the spotlight. So it was only fitting that the 1932 Olympic Games, the scene of her greatest triumph, would be held not only in her home country, but in Los Angeles, the land of movie stars, dreams, and celebrities.

On to the Olympics

At the Olympic qualifying meet in 1932, Babe Didrikson competed as a one-person team representing Employers Casualty. Entering eight of the ten events, she won gold medals in six of them, earning a meet-high score of thirty points. The second place team—consisting of twenty-two women from the University of Illinois—together scored twenty-two points.

Olympic rules limited Babe to competing in only three events. So for the big stage in L.A., she chose three events in which she had set world records during the qualifying meet—the high

Didrikson (right) on her way to gold in the 80-meter hurdles at the 1932 Olympics.

jump, the 80-meter hurdles, and the javelin throw.

On the train ride from Texas to the L.A. Olympics, Babe annoyed her teammates, who thought her behavior to be crass and unladylike. She played the harmonica loudly, exercised in the aisles of the cramped railroad car, and bragged about her greatness.

When the train arrived in Los Angeles, though, Babe Didrikson was treated with all the fanfare of a superstar. The press loved her self-assuredness and her ability to entertain an audience, even as she outraged her teammates. When asked if she would win, Babe replied to a crowded room full of reporters, "I came out here to beat everybody in sight, and that's just what I'm going to do!"

True to her word, on her very first try, in her very first event, Babe Didrikson shattered the Olympic record in the javelin throw by over 11 feet (3.36 meters), capturing her first Olympic gold medal, with a toss of 143 feet 4 inches (43.72 m).

In her next event, the 80-meter hurdles, Babe tied the world record of 11.8 seconds in the first heat. But the best was yet to come. Following a false start, which disqualified her from the second heat, Babe broke the world record with a time of 11.7 seconds.

Her U.S. teammate Evelyne Hall was also clocked at 11.7 seconds and sported a welt on her neck which she claimed came from breaking the tape before Babe. But after a debate among the judges, the gold medal and the world record was given to Babe Didrikson. How the judges came to this decision is not known, but they did give Hall joint credit for the world record.

Controversy surrounded Babe's final event as well. In the high jump, she tied her U.S. teammate Jean Shiley at a world-record height of 5 feet 5 ¼ inches (1.66 m). Both athletes missed the next height of 5 feet 6 inches (1.68 m), so the bar was reset to 5 feet 5 ¼ inches for a runoff. Again both Didrikson and Shiley cleared the bar, but this time the judges ruled that Babe used an illegal jumping style, going over head-first—a style common today, but against the rules in 1932—and the gold medal was awarded to Shiley, much to the delight of her teammates.

OLYMPIC STATS

Stats for the top five finishers in the three events in which Babe Didrikson competed in the 1932 Olympics

	Athlete	Country	Distance
Javelin Throw	1. Mildred "Babe" Didrikson	United States	143' 4" (43.72 meters), gold medal, Olympic record
	2. Ellen Braumüller	Germany	142' 8" (43.51 meters), silver medal
	3. Ottilie "Tilly" Fleischer	Germany	141' 1" (43 meters), bronze medal
	4. Masako Shimpo	Japan	128' 2" (39.09 meters)
	5. Nan Gindele	United States	124' 6" (37.97 meters)
80-Meter Hurdles	1. Mildred "Babe" Didrikson	United States	11.7 seconds, gold medal, world record
	2. Evelyne Hall	United States	11.7 seconds, silver medal, world record
	3. Marjorie Clark	South Africa	11.8 seconds, bronze medal
	4. Simone Schaller	United States	11.9 seconds
	5. Violet Webb	Great Britain	11.9 seconds
High Jump	1. Jean Shiley	United States	5' 5 ¼" (1.66 meters), gold medal, world record
	2. Mildred "Babe" Didrikson	United States	5' 5 ¼" (1.66 meters), silver medal, world record
	3. Eva Dawes	Canada	5' 3" (1.6 meters), bronze medal
	4. Carolina Gisolf	Holland	5' 2 ¼" (1.58 meters)
	5. Marjorie Clark	South Africa	5' 2 ¼" (1.58 meters)

Babe took the silver medal, but did retain a share of the new world record.

Among all her incredible achievements, Babe Didrikson's performance at the 1932 Olympics stands out as one of sport's shining moments: two gold medals, one silver medal, two world records, and an Olympic record. She had also become the first athlete ever to win individual medals in running, throwing, and jumping events.

Didrikson is neck and neck at the 80-meter-hurdles finish line with Evelyne Hall.

Continued Fame

Following her Olympic triumph, Babe stayed in the limelight, touring the country with men's baseball teams, striking out stunned male players, and even pitching in exhibition games for the major-league Brooklyn Dodgers and St. Louis Cardinals. On December 23, 1938, she married George Zaharias, a professional wrestler.

In 1944, Babe Didrikson Zaharias brought

After her Olympic glory, Didrikson went on to become a champion golfer and a founder of the LPGA.

her ferocious competitive fire to the world of women's golf. She quickly established herself as the top women's golfer in the world, at one point winning seventeen consecutive amateur tournaments. She turned pro in 1948, and in the following year, she helped establish the Ladies Professional Golf Association (LPGA).

Babe won two U.S. Women's Open Golf Championships (1948, 1950) before being diagnosed with colon cancer in 1953. Following surgery and time away for recovery, Babe picked up her clubs again in 1954 and won her third U.S. Open Championship.

Two years later, the cancer returned and cut her life tragically short, claiming this great champion at the age of forty-two. It can be said that Babe Didrikson's life itself was one of the great shining moments not only in women's sports but in the history of athletic competition.

THREE-TIME CHAMP

Sonja Henie Charms the Judges at the 1936 Olympics

Flashing across the ice like none before her, leaping and spinning, dancing and flying, Sonja Henie single-handedly revolution-ized and popularized the sport of figure skat-ing, once the exclusive domain of rich men.

Born in Oslo, Norway, in 1912, Sonja Henie started dance lessons almost as soon as she could walk. This early training would profoundly affect her skat-ing in the years to come.

Receiving her first pair of skates at the age of six, young Sonja told her parents when she was ten, "I want to win the world's championship." Her well-to-do father threw his support behind her, hiring the best skating and dance teachers to help the young athlete develop. It was the inclusion of ballet tech-niques that would allow Henie to change the sport forever.

At the 1928 Olympics in St. Moritz, sixteen-year-old Sonja Henie surprised the world by winning the gold.

Young Olympian

Sonja Henie competed in the 1924 Olympics in Chamonix, France, at the age of eleven. Although she finished eighth out of eight competitors, her bold display of agility, strength, and confidence made a last-ing impression on the world of skating. The judges were so taken with her talent and style that, despite her last-place overall finish, the eleven-year-old placed third in the more creative freestyle portion of the event.

Practicing intensely for the next two

years, Sonja competed in the world championships in 1926, finishing second. It would be the last time she ever lost a competition.

In 1927, at the age of fifteen, Henie took her innovative blend of athletic spins and jumps, and graceful classical dance choreography to the world championships. She won the first of what would turn out to be ten consecutive world championships.

At the 1928 Winter Olympics in St. Moritz, Switzerland, Henie captured six of the seven first-place votes to win her first Olympic gold medal. Her inventive, balletic style, coupled with spins, jumps, and turns, marked the first time a well-choreographed dance routine had been incorporated into a freestyle program in Olympic competition, while still meeting all of the competition's technical requirements.

By the time the 1932 Olympics were held in Lake Placid, New York, young skaters had already begun to imitate Henie's revolutionary approach to the sport. Two eleven-year-olds from England, Megan Taylor and Cecilia Colledge, attempted Henie-like choreography in their routines and finished a respectable seventh and eighth in the competition. But it was Henie who captured Olympic gold for the second time, the unanimous first-place choice of the seven judges.

At the 1936 Games

By 1936, Sonja Henie was a worldwide superstar. She was so popular that wherever she traveled—

Sonja Henie during her figure-skating routine at the 1936 Olympics, where she won her third consecutive gold medal.

from New York to Prague to Paris—the police had to be called out to control the adoring crowds.

Just before the 1936 Olympics in Garmisch-Partenkirchen, Germany, Henie announced that she would retire from competitive skating following the 1936 world championships, which were to take place one week after the Olympics. Wanting to close out her stunning career with an unprecedented third consecutive Olympic gold medal, Henie felt self-imposed pressure heading into the Games.

Going into the all-important free-skating program, Henie held a slim 3.6-point lead over Britain's Cecilia Colledge—one of the young skaters who had based her routines on Henie's innovations. As she glided out onto the ice for her free skate, Colledge pandered to the German crowd by flashing a Nazi salute, a nod to the Nazi Party that controlled Germany, and its leader, Adolf Hitler. Moments before Colledge began her routine, it was discovered that someone had prepared the wrong music for her. The skater was flustered and angry during the tense minutes of delay while the correct music was found, and those emotions affected her performance. She fell during the first minute of her routine but recovered enough to score a 5.7 out of a possible 6 points.

Henie was the final skater of the competition, and she appeared nervous as she hit the ice. But she called on her experience and athletic ability to pull off a solid performance, good enough for a score of 5.8 and her third consecutive Olympic gold medal—a record that has still never been matched.

Skating Star

Following her tenth consecutive world championship one week later, Sonja Henie retired from competition. She set out on her professional career, starring in enormously popular ice shows

OLYMPIC STATS

Stats for the top five finishers in the three Olympic Games in which Sonja Henie won gold medals

	Athlete	Country	Points
1928 Olympics—	1. Sonja Henie	Norway	2452.25, gold medal
St. Moritz, Switzerland	2. Fritzi Burger	Austria	2254.50, silver medal
	3. Beatrix Loughran	United States	2248.50, bronze medal
	4. Maribel Vinson	United States	2224.50
	5. Cecil Smith	Canada	2213.75
1932 Olympics—	1. Sonja Henie	Norway	2302.5, gold medal
Lake Placid, New York	2. Fritzi Burger	Austria	2167.1, silver medal
	3. Maribel Vinson	United States	2158.5, bronze medal
	4. Constance Wilson-Samuel	Canada	2131.9
	5. Vivi-Anne Hultén	Sweden	2129.5
1936 Olympics—	1. Sonja Henie	Norway	425.5, gold medal
Garmisch-Partenkirchen,	2. Cecilia Colledge	Great Britain	418.1, silver medal
Germany	3. Vivi-Anne Hultén	Sweden	394.7, bronze medal
	4. Liselotte Landbeck	Belgium	393.3
	5. Maribel Vinson	United States	388.7

that toured the United States. While in Los Angeles for an ice show, movie executive Darryl F. Zanuck caught her performance and offered her a contract. A string of successful movies followed in the 1930s and 1940s.

Not only did Sonja Henie win three straight Olympic gold medals and entertain millions through her movies during the Great Depression, but she popularized the sport of ice-skating for the masses. Following her success and popularity, hundreds of ice rinks popped up all across the United States, and thousands of girls took up the sport, dreaming of one day leaping and flying across the ice just like Sonja Henie.

KATARINA WITT

The closest any skater has come to matching Sonja Henie's three consecutive Olympic gold medals is Katarina Witt of the former East Germany. Witt always attracted attention with her flashy, athletic style, privileged attitude, and controversial, provocative costumes. She won back-to-back Olympic gold in 1984 and 1988, becoming the first skater to accomplish that feat since Sonja Henie did it in 1928 and 1932.

After retiring from competition, Henie became a star of both ice shows and the movies.

CHANGING PERCEPTIONS

The All-American Girls Professional Baseball League

It was a time of war, a time of extraordinary events occurring around the globe and back home in the United States. The year was 1943, and America had been deeply involved in World War II for two years. Virtually every able-bodied young man in the nation had been drafted into the armed forces.

As a result, many jobs previously thought to be "man's work" were now being done by women. Rosie the Riveter—an illustrated character popularized in posters and newsreels— became a symbol of women's ability to do the jobs once thought the exclusive territory of men. With her sleeves rolled up and her muscles showing, Rosie sat high atop a construction site firing rivets into

The camera catches Chicago Colleens pitcher Jean Marlowe in her windup at spring training.

steel girders—and she did it as well as any man.

All the men who played major-league baseball were not exempt from the long arm of the draft. In fact, many players volunteered to serve in the armed forces. The pool of major-league talent was greatly depleted as many of its top stars—including Ted Williams, Hank Greenberg, and Joe DiMaggio—went off to war.

Forming the League

Into this atmosphere stepped Philip K. Wrigley, owner of the major-league Chicago Cubs and the Wrigley's Chewing Gum Company. Worried that baseball fans would lose interest in the game while its male stars were away, Wrigley sent scouts all over

Kenosha Comets Shirley Jamison (with her foot on the bag) and Ann Harnett during practice.

the United States and Canada, searching for the best women softball players. Using the lesson of Rosie the Riveter, Wrigley figured that if women could work construction, drive buses, and do other traditionally male jobs, they could play baseball for fans of the national pastime.

More than forty thousand women already played semipro softball in small towns across America. Wrigley gathered the best of those players and formed the first women's professional baseball league. The All-American Girls Softball League, as it was originally called, was formed in 1943 with teams in four Midwestern cities: the Racine Belles, the Kenosha Comets, the South Bend Blue Sox, and the Rockford Peaches.

The league was an instant hit, drawing more than two hundred thousand fans during its inaugural season. In the beginning, it was still a softball league, complete with underhand pitching and a larger ball. As the league progressed, and after World War II ended in 1945, the game switched to traditional baseball, with overhand pitching, a smaller ball, and greater distance between the bases. In 1948, the league changed its name to the All-American Girls Professional Baseball League (AAGPBL) and added teams in Minneapolis, Fort Wayne, Grand Rapids, Battle Creek, Kalamazoo, and Springfield. Clearly, Philip Wrigley was right. The league was a tremendous success, drawing close to one million fans in 1948.

Former hockey star Eddie Stumpf, shown here as coach of the Rockford Peaches, gives a pep talk to a group of his players (from left to right): Elise Harney, Lois Florreich, Mille Warwick, Olive Little, and Dottie Green.

The players wore uniforms that included short skirts and gym shorts. These outfits were clearly designed to appeal to male patrons, but they didn't offer much protection against the scrapes that came with base running and stealing. Concerned that the players maintain their "femininity" while displaying athletic prowess, Wrigley insisted that the women of the AAGPBL go to a charm school he set up to learn etiquette and proper makeup techniques. Players could not wear slacks, shorts, or jeans in public, nor could they cut their hair short. Each team had a chaperon to accompany the women when they enjoyed a night out while on the road. Wrigley worked hard to ensure that the "ladylike" image that was the social norm of the time was maintained by all the players in his league.

Baseball fans came to love the play of these talented women—who sacrificed nothing in the way of skill to keep up their "proper" images—and packed the stands to root for their favorites. Among the standouts who captured the fans' interest were Jean Faut, who pitched two perfect games; Joanne Weaver, who hit .429 one season; and Sophie Kurys, who averaged 100 stolen bases a season and in one year stole 201 bases in 203 attempts—still the single-season record for professional baseball.

The End of the League

By 1950, with the war over and major-league players returning, league attendance began to drop. The return of men from war, the growing popularity of television, specifically televised major-league baseball games, and the postwar American view that a woman's place was in the home—not at home plate—led to the league's demise in 1954. Suburbia was on the rise; the baby boom was in full swing; and Rosie the Riveter, while remembered fondly by some and as a necessary evil by others, handed her tools back to the men.

Elise Harney, a pitcher for the Kenosha Comets, applies makeup between innings as her teammates look on.

The All-American Girls Professional Baseball League hit the big screen in the 1992 film A League of Their Own.

Still, the importance of the AAGPBL cannot be overlooked. For more than a decade, the United States supported a professional women's sports league that thrived, showcasing talent and entertaining millions of fans. AAGPBL players forever changed the belief that women couldn't play a tough, aggressive brand of baseball.

The league's 1945 batting champ, Helen Callaghan, recalled years later what the experience meant to her personally: "I was just a little girl, miles from home, and this experience allowed me to be independent, to have my own money, and to make my own decisions at a time when few women did that. Women were supposed to be in the kitchen, taking care of kids. They weren't supposed to be considered independent people. That was what was so great about the league. We got to make choices."

BEFORE THE AAGPBL

Women's involvement in baseball goes back almost to the beginning of the game in the early 1800s. In 1866, freshmen women at Vassar College formed a baseball team with the support of a female physician who thought the exercise would be good for the young women.

But the team didn't last long. Following several injuries to players, the school banned the game. College baseball for women resurfaced in 1880 at Smith College, but again this "overly violent" activity was soon put to a stop.

In the late 1800s, showmen and promoters began to send teams of baseball-playing women around the country to play before local crowds. During this practice—known as "barnstorming"—women's teams played against each other, or occasionally the top female talent played against men.

By the 1890s, barnstorming "bloomer" girls—named for the long, loose-fitting bloomer-like uniforms they wore—were crisscrossing the country playing baseball and drawing huge crowds.

In the early 1900s, a young woman from Ohio named Alta Weiss began pitching for boys' teams when she was fourteen years old. By age sixteen, she had joined a men's semipro team and was soon dominating male batters with her astounding pitching skill, playing before crowds of more than three thousand spectators.

Using the money she made from showing off her baseball skills, Alta Weiss put herself through medical school. She continued to play off and on, even as she practiced medicine, well into the 1920s.

BREAKING RECORDS

Wilma Rudolph's Success at the 1960 Olympics

Wilma Rudolph's unprecedented performance at the 1960 Olympic Games was an amazing achievement by any standards. With her blinding speed and astonishing strength of will, Rudolph became the first American woman to win three gold medals in track and field at a single Olympics, setting world records in two of the events.

During the opening heat of the 200-meter race at the 1960 Olympic Games, Wilma Rudolph set a world record time of 22.9 seconds.

But Wilma Rudolph's stunning victories are even more incredible when you consider the obstacles she had to overcome just to stand up and walk on her own, much less claim the title of the "World's Fastest Woman."

Overcoming Obstacles

As a young child, Wilma suffered from double pneumonia, scarlet fever, and polio. This triple assault on her young, fragile body left her with a partially paralyzed left leg. Doctors said that Wilma would never walk normally, but she and her family persisted. Her mother took her for treatments and physical therapy, and her ten brothers and sisters gave her daily massages.

Wilma used leg braces and orthopedic shoes to help her walk until the age of twelve; then the braces and special shoes came off, and Wilma Rudolph began to play basketball with her brothers. She soon proved to be a phenom on the neighborhood basketball courts in her hometown of Clarksville, Tennessee.

In high school, Rudolph starred on the basketball team, setting a single-season scoring record in her sophomore year. She also got involved in track and field, where she specialized in sprinting, winning the state high school titles in the 50-, 75-, and 100-yard (45.7-, 68.6-, and 91.4-m) dashes.

At age fifteen in 1955, Wilma began practicing with the Tennessee State track team—tops in the nation—under the watchful eye of legendary track coach Ed Temple. The following year, through sheer determination and endless hard work, Wilma Rudolph earned a spot on the U.S. Olympic track team. At the 1956 Olympics, at age sixteen, she and her teammates earned a bronze medal in the

4 x 100-meter relay race. But that was merely a prelude.

Capturing Gold

Four years later, at the 1960 Olympics in Rome, Italy, Wilma Rudolph shattered expectations and world records, electrifying the spectators with her speed and grace and taking her place as the world's fastest woman.

In the semifinal heat of the 100-meter dash, Rudolph tied the world record of 11.3 seconds, crossing the finish line a full 3 yards (2.7 m) ahead of her closest competitor. Her margin of victory was the same in the final, but her speed was an astounding 11 seconds flat. Although Rudolph claimed her first gold medal in the race, she was denied the world record for her 11.0 finish because the wind at her back was over the Olympic limit of 2 miles (3.2 kilometers) per hour.

Rudolph (far right) crosses the finish line in the 200—and takes the gold—with a time of 24 seconds.

In the 100-meter race, Rudolph took another gold, while Dorothy Hyman of Great Britain won a silver and Giuseppina Leone of Italy brought home the bronze.

Up next was the 200-meter dash, in which Rudolph set a world record with a time of 22.9 seconds in a qualifying heat, the first time a woman had ever broken the 23-second barrier. She then went on to grab her second gold medal with a 24.0 time in the final, a full four-tenths of a second faster than the silver medalist, a huge margin of victory in so short a race.

Rudolph's final event was the 4 x 100-meter relay race, the event in which she had won a bronze medal four years earlier, running the third leg of the race. This time, Wilma ran the all-important fourth and final leg of the relay.

As Wilma's teammate Barbara Jordan completed the third leg of the race, she held a 2-yard (1.8-m) lead for the U.S. team. But a sloppy baton pass from Jordan to Rudolph cost the U.S. team the lead.

Calling on reserves of strength and depth of spirit, Wilma Rudolph retook the lead for good as she swept around the track for the final time, clinching her third gold medal of the Games and helping her teammates to set a new world record with a time of 44.5 seconds.

Rudolph's success at the 1960 Olympics, the first Olympic Games to be viewed by a television audience of millions, represented a huge step forward in the acceptance of women's athletics in the United States. Thousands of girls who watched her tearing around the track on TV were inspired to join local track clubs or to demand competitive athletic opportunities in their schools.

The seeds of Title IX had been planted.

Track star Wilma Rudolph proudly displaying her three Olympic gold medals.

OLYMPIC STATS

Stats for the top five finishers in the three Olympic events in which
Wilma Rudolph won gold medals at the 1960 Olympics in Rome

	Athlete	Country	Time
100-Meter Dash	1. Wilma Rudolph	United States	11.0 seconds, gold medal[1]
	2. Dorothy Hyman	Great Britain	11.3 seconds, silver medal[2]
	3. Giuseppina Leone	Italy	11.3 seconds, bronze medal
	4. Maria Itkina	Soviet Union	11.4 seconds
	5. Catherine Capdeville	France	11.5 seconds
200-Meter Dash	1. Wilma Rudolph	United States	24.0 seconds, gold medal
	2. Jutta Heine	Germany[3]	24.4 seconds, silver medal
	3. Dorothy Hyman	Germany	24.7 seconds, bronze medal[4]
	4. Maria Itkina	Soviet Union	24.7 seconds
	5. Barbara Janiszewska	Poland	24.8 seconds
4 x 100-Meter Relay	1. Martha Hudson, Lucinda Williams, Barbara Jordan, Wilma Rudolph	United States	44.5 seconds, gold medal, world record
	2. Martha Langbein, Annie Biechl, Brunhilde Hendrix, Jutta Heine	Germany	44.8 seconds, silver medal
	3. Teresa Wieczorek, Barbara Janiszewska, Celina Jesionowska, Halina Richter	Poland	45.0 seconds, bronze medal
	4. Vyera Krepkina, Valentina Maslovskaya, Maria Itkina, Iryna Press	Soviet Union	45.2 seconds
	5. Letizia Bertoni, Sandra Valenti, Piera Tizzoni, Giuseppina Leone	Italy	45.6 seconds

[1] World record time not counted due to wind conditions.
[2] .05 seconds faster than the third-place finisher.
[3] Teams from East and West Germany competed as a unified team in 1960.
[4] .03 seconds faster than the fourth-place finisher.

Chapter FIVE

MARATHON MIRACLE

Joan Benoit Samuelson at the 1984 Olympics

It takes almost super-human strength, conditioning, stamina, and mental toughness to run the 26 miles, 385 yards (42 km) of a marathon race in just over two hours. From the time of the first modern Olympics in 1896 until the 1984 Games in Los Angeles, it was widely believed that women didn't have what it took to complete this arduous task in the Olympic Games. Joan Benoit Samuelson shattered that belief forever.

Joan Benoit Samuelson with a strong first-place finish at the 1979 Boston Marathon.

All-Round Athlete

A natural athlete, Joan Benoit Samuelson played tennis, basketball, lacrosse, and field hockey as a child, but her first love when it came to sports was skiing, an activity she excelled at almost from the time she could walk.

After breaking a leg while skiing during her senior year of high school, Benoit Samuelson took up running to get back into shape. She immediately discovered a new athletic passion.

One year later, she had progressed enough to qualify for a Junior Olympics track competition.

Beginning in 1976, Benoit Samuelson attended college and played several sports, but she primarily focused on her running. In 1979, running in only her second marathon, she won the world's most famous long-distance race, the legendary Boston Marathon, establishing a new U.S. women's record with a time of 2:35:15.

For the next few years, Benoit Samuelson worked as a track coach at Boston University, training alongside her students. In 1983, with her sights set firmly on the first Olympic women's marathon to be held the following year, she devoted herself full time to running. That year she won her second Boston Marathon, this time setting a new world record of 2:22:43.

As 1984 dawned, Benoit Samuelson began running 100 miles (160.9 km) per week to prepare for the Games that summer. Then, two and half weeks before the Olympic trials in May, something snapped in

Benoit Samuelson took an early lead in the 1984 Olympic Marathon, and she held it all the way to the finish line.

her right knee, and she underwent arthroscopic surgery. The day after the surgery, she pedaled an exercise bike with her hands to keep her cardio-vascular system operating at training level. Two days later she was walking on a treadmill, and four days after that she was running again. Just seventeen days after knee surgery, Joan Benoit Samuelson won the Olympic trial.

Making History

As the first women's marathon in Olympic history began, many spectators lining the route wept with joy as the lengthy struggle to achieve recognition for women's long-distance running finally bore fruit. Just fourteen minutes into the race, Joan Benoit Samuelson pulled away from the field of runners and never looked back. No one came close to her.

Her nearest rival, Norway's Grete Waitz—who would come to dominate the New York Marathon—ran a distant second. She thought that Benoit Samuelson's early push would come

Benoit Samuelson's closest competition in the Olympics was Norway's Grete Waitz (shown leading Laura Fogli of Italy and Ingrid Kristiansen of Norway), who went on to win silver.

back to haunt her in the final grueling miles of the race, but she was wrong. Benoit Samuelson never relinquished the lead.

One half mile from the Los Angeles Coliseum, where the long race would finally end, and where more than fifty thousand screaming fans awaited her arrival, Benoit Samuelson passed a huge mural illustrating her victory at the Boston Marathon. Entering the tunnel leading to the coliseum's track, where she would complete her final lap and through her actions announce to the world that women belonged

OLYMPIC STATS

Stats for the top five finishers in the 1984 Women's Olympic Marathon

Athlete	Country	Time
1. Joan Benoit Samuelson	United States	2:24:52, gold medal
2. Grete Waitz	Norway	2:26:18, silver medal
3. Rosa Mota	Portugal	2:26:57, bronze medal
4. Ingrid Kristiansen	Norway	2:27:34
5. Lorraine Moller	New Zealand	2:28:34

among the ranks of great long-distance runners, Benoit Samuelson thought to herself, "When you come out from underneath the tunnel, you're going to be different person." She would be different, and the world of long-distance running would never be the same.

As she burst onto the track, the massive throng stood as one and cheered the lone figure as she finished the race 400 meters and more than one minute ahead of the rest of the pack.

Joan Benoit Samuelson's gold medal time of 2:24:52 not only was the third-best time ever run by a woman in a marathon but would actually have taken the gold medal in thirteen of the previous twenty Olympic marathons run by men!

TIMELESS SPIRIT

At the first modern Olympics held in Athens, Greece, in 1896, women were not allowed to compete in the Olympic race. The race was held on April 10 and measured 42 kilometers, running from the city of Marathon (from which the long-distance race would eventually take its name) to Athens. That didn't stop a woman named Melpomene from running the course on March 6 of that year in a time of four hours, thirty minutes.

On April 11, the day after the official race had been run, another woman, Stamata Revithi, set out from Marathon in the early morning and arrived in Athens five hours, thirty minutes later, having stopped along the way to watch a fleet of ships go by.

A victorious Joan Benoit Samuelson relishes her victory lap.

A GOLDEN YEAR

Steffi Graf Wins the Olympic Gold and the Grand Slam

It was a year like no other in tennis history, an achievement like few others in the history of sports. In 1988, nineteen-year-old Steffi Graf of Germany became only the third woman in history to win professional tennis's four major tournaments—the Australian Open, the French Open, Wimbledon, and the U.S. Open, collectively known as the Grand Slam of tennis—all in the same year.

Then, to top off her fairy-tale year, Graff traveled to Seoul, South

Steffi Graf, one of tennis's all-time greats.

Korea, where she captured the gold medal for tennis at the 1988 Olympic Games. During that magical year, Steffi Graf won seventy-two of the seventy-five matches she played.

The Road to Number One

This incredible year was the culmination of Graf's professional career, which had started in 1982 when she was thirteen years old. By 1985, she began to make a name for herself in women's tennis, ranking sixth in the world. Early the following year, Graf made headlines by defeating Chris Evert, the sport's top athlete and biggest star, for her first major tournament victory.

In 1987, Graf finally reached the coveted number-one ranking among all women's tennis players, a position she held for an astounding, record-breaking 186 consecutive weeks. That year she beat Evert, then Martina Navratilova—another longtime champion—in back-to-back matches in a tournament in Florida, then went on to win her first Grand Slam tournament, defeating Navratilova in the 1987 French Open.

From Melbourne to Paris to London

As great as 1987 was for Steffi Graf, 1988 would prove to be even more spectacular. One characteristic of a true tennis champion is the ability to play well on all different types of court surfaces. This would be necessary for Graf to succeed in her quest for four victories in four tournaments played on a variety of surfaces.

Her golden Grand Slam year began in January at the Australian Open in Melbourne, playing on rubberized hard court, a tough, fast surface. She defeated Chris Evert 6–1, 7–6 to capture her first Grand Slam title of the year.

The French Open was next. Playing on red clay, a much slower surface, Graf had to adjust her game and tempo. She cruised to victory in France beating Soviet star Natalia Zvereva 6–0, 6–0.

That July, at Wimbledon in England—the most famous, longest-running tennis tournament in the world—Graf battled Navratilova in a titanic struggle on the natural grass surface. Navratilova, the reigning Wimbledon champ, took the first set from Graf by a score of 7–5. A victory in the second set would have given Navratilova her seventh consecutive Wimbledon

On her way to a perfect season, Graf proudly displays her 1988 Wimbledon trophy.

Graf is set to serve at the 1988 U.S. Open at Flushing Meadows, New York.

Capturing the Slam and the Gold

At the U.S. Open, the final jewel in the Grand Slam crown, the flags of four nations—Australia, France, England, and the United States—flew above the tennis stadium, representing Graf's three previous victories and her quest for a fourth, there in New York.

At this tournament, Graf was back on hard court. Most of her opponents in the early rounds of the U.S. Open admitted later that they were afraid even to step onto the court with Graf, so strong was her game at that point, so fierce her desire to win. Breezing to the final match,

title. But Graf battled back, taking the second set 6–2, then the third and deciding set 6–1 to capture the tournament.

Graf faced her own doubles partner, Argentine teenager Gabriela Sabatini, for the title. Sabatini had already beaten Graf twice earlier that year.

After taking the first set 6–3, Graf was overpowered by Sabatini in the second set, which the Argentine won 6–3. When Sabatini won the first point of the final and deciding set, it looked as if Steffi Graf's dream of a Grand Slam might be slipping from her grasp.

Pulling herself together, Graf went on a tear. Using all her skill and power, she won eight straight points and fifteen of the next seventeen, capturing the final set 6–1 against the exhausted Sabatini and winning the U.S. Open to complete her Grand Slam.

Within a few days of her victory in New York, Graf flew to Korea, where she captured the Olympic gold medal, once again beating Gabriela Sabatini in the finals, this time in straight sets of 6–3 and 6–3.

Steffi Graf continued to dominate women's tennis through 1996, but she will always be best remembered for 1988, the year of her golden Grand Slam.

ALTHEA GIBSON SHATTERS TENNIS'S COLOR BARRIER

In the 1950s, African-American tennis players were barred from private country clubs around the United States—where the best players received training from the top coaches—as well as from major tournaments. In spite of this injustice, a talented young African-American woman named Althea Gibson did not let the racial barriers stop her. As a child, she enjoyed playing table tennis in Harlem recreational programs. This interest eventually led to tennis, and she trained on public courts that were open to African-Americans.

In 1950, twenty-three-year-old Gibson became the first African-American—man or woman—to play in a major U.S. Lawn Tennis Association event, one held at the West Side Tennis Club in New York. She lost to former Wimbledon champ Louise Brough.

In 1956, another barrier fell when Gibson won the French Open, becoming the first black player to capture a Grand Slam title. The following year she became the first African-American to win Wimbledon, a title she took again in 1958.

Battling racism at every turn in the white-dominated world of tennis, Althea Gibson's courage and talent opened the door for great players of all races to show their abilities on the court. Her victories at Wimbledon stand as great moments for the world of sports, for women athletes, and for African-American athletes.

ABOVE AND BEYOND

Jackie Joyner-Kersee at the 1988 Olympics

Just as Babe Didrikson Zaharias was considered the finest female athlete of the first half of the twentieth century, there is little doubt that Jackie Joyner-Kersee was the finest of the latter half. "I like the heptathlon," Jackie Joyner-Kersee was quoted as saying, "because it shows what you are made of." What this extraordinary athlete is made of is an intense desire to win, incredible athletic ability, and tremendous passion for her sport.

Jackie Joyner-Kersee at the 1988 Olympics, preparing for the javelin throw, just one of seven events that make up the heptathlon.

The most physically and mentally demanding part of a track-and-field competition, the heptathlon is made up of seven events—the 200-meter dash, the 100-meter hurdles, the high jump, the shot put, the long jump, the javelin throw, and the 800-meter run—held over a two-day period.

At the 1988 Olympics in Seoul, South Korea, Jackie Joyner-Kersee took achievement in the world of track and field to a new level, taking the gold medal in the heptathlon, setting a world record in the event with an astounding 7,291 points, breaking the rarely surpassed 7,000 point level, and finishing nearly 400 points ahead of her nearest competitor. Joyner-Kersee followed up her record-setting performance in the heptathlon by capturing the gold medal in the long jump event five days later, setting an Olympic record with a jump of 7.4 meters.

The Beginning of Greatness

Jackie Joyner-Kersee's road to Seoul and her astounding performances at the 1988 Olympics began in a poverty-stricken neighborhood in East St. Louis, Illinois. At the age of nine, Jackie Joyner entered her first track competition, finishing last. With the help and encouragement of her parents and her brother Al (who would himself win a gold medal in the triple jump at the 1984 Olympics), Jackie continued competing and soon specialized in the long jump.

At age fourteen, Jackie took up the five-event pentathlon and told her family that she wanted to compete in the Olympics one day. In high school, she excelled in sports and participated in volleyball, basketball, and track and field. In 1981, she started working with coach Bob Kersee (who would remain her coach and in 1986 become her husband), focusing on the heptathlon and the high jump. At the 1984 Olympics in Los Angeles, Joyner placed fifth in the high jump and took the silver medal in the heptathlon, finishing just five points behind the winner.

Olympic Success

The memory of her close but disappointing second-place finish in the heptathlon in 1984 fueled Joyner-Kersee's drive to win in 1988. As the competition began, she jumped out to a large lead on the first day, setting a personal-best time of 12.69 seconds in the 100-meter hurdles. On day two, she set a heptathlon world record in the long jump at 7.27 meters, and a personal best of 2:06.51 seconds in the 800-meters. When it was all over, Jackie Joyner-Kersee had run away with the gold medal and a new world record.

Joyner-Kersee on her way to 7.40 meters, enough to win the long jump competition.

Five days later, while competing in the high jump, she trailed going into the fifth and final jump. The leader, Heike Drechsler of East Germany, had jumped 7.22 meters. Joyner-Kersee's best jump to this point was a 7.16. From the sideline, Bob Kersee called out, "You have a 7.40 in you!" Inspired by the encouragement, Jackie Joyner-Kersee focused on keeping her knees high and staying in the air for as long as possible in her final jump. Bob Kersee was right. Jackie took the gold with a jump of exactly 7.40 meters, tying an Olympic record and completing one of the great triumphs in Olympic history.

Following her second Olympic gold medal

OLYMPIC STATS

Stats for the top five finishers in the two events in which Jackie Joyner-Kersee won the gold medal at the 1988 Olympics

Heptathlon:

Athlete/Country medal/record	100m H seconds	HJ meters	SP meters	200M seconds	LJ meters	JT meters	800M min:sec	Total Points
1. Jackie Joyner-Kersee United States gold medal/world record	12.69	1.86	15.80	22.56	7.27	45.66	2:06.51	7291
2. Sabine John East Germany silver medal	12.85	1.80	16.23	23.65	6.71	42.56	2:06.14	6897
3. Anke Behmer East Germany bronze medal	13.20	1.83	14.20	23.10	6.68	44.45	2:04.20	6858
4. Natalya Shubenkova Soviet Union/Russia	13.51	1.74	14.76	23.93	6.32	47.46	2:07.90	6540
5. Remigia Sablovskaite Soviet Union/Lithuania	13.61	1.80	15.23	23.92	6.25	42.78	2:12.24	6456

Key to events: 100m H = 100-meter hurdles, HJ = high jump, SP = shot put, 200M = 200-meter dash, LJ = long jump, JT = javelin throw, 800M = 800-meter run

Long Jump:	Athlete	Country	Distance
	1. Jackie Joyner-Kersee	United States	7.40 meters, gold medal
	2. Heike Drechsler	East Germany	7.22 meters, silver medal
	3. R. Galina Čistjaková	Soviet Union/Russia	7.11 meters, bronze medal
	4. Olena Belevska	Soviet Union/Russia	7.04 meters
	5. Nicole Boegman	Australia	6.73 meters

in the heptathlon four years later in Barcelona, Spain, Joyner-Kersee looked back on her place in history. She thought about the lasting legacy of her courage, stamina, and determination, as well as the influence she has had as an inspiration to the next generation of female track-and-field athletes.

"I remember where I came from," she said, referring to the East St. Louis ghetto in which she grew up, "and I keep that in mind. If a young female sees the environment I grew up in and sees my dreams and goals come true, they will realize their dreams and goals might also come true."

Heptathlon champion Joyner-Kersee enjoying her moment of victory.

FLO-JO

They couldn't have been more different in style. Jackie Joyner-Kersee was all muscle and sweat. Her sister-in-law and fellow gold medalist in track and field at the 1988 Olympics, Florence Griffith Joyner, known to the world as "Flo-Jo," was all flashy glitter, sexy outfits, and outrageous fingernails and makeup.

What they had in common, other than the fact that Flo-Jo married Jackie's brother Al Joyner, was phenomenal ability and heart. Flo-Jo flashed onto the scene at the Olympic trials in 1988, smashing the world record in the 100-meter dash, earning the title of the "World's Fastest Woman."

Teamed with Jackie Joyner-Kersee on the U.S. Olympic track team in Seoul, Flo-Jo took the gold in the 100-meter dash, the 200-meter dash, and the 4 x 100-meter relay, earning three gold medals while her sister-in-law brought home two. Their friendship, contrast in styles, and superb athleticism captured the imagination of sports fans around the world.

In 1996, Flo-Jo suffered a seizure during a plane flight. She was hospitalized for one day. Two years later, she suffered another seizure, this one affecting her heart, and she died at the early age of thirty-eight.

STAYING POWER

Martina Navratilova Wins Her Ninth Wimbledon Tournament

Martina Navratilova's concentration and athleticism helped her capture her ninth Wimbledon championship in 1990.

Shortly after being named the Female Athlete of the Decade for the 1980s by the National Sports Review, the Associated Press, and United Press International, Martina Navratilova began the new decade with a victory at the Wimbledon tennis tournament. This triumph was Navratilova's ninth Wimbledon singles title, and it set a new record, surpassing the record of eight Wimbledon titles set by Helen Wills Moody in 1938. This achievement, which elevated Martina Navratilova to the status of the all-time greatest player in women's tennis, stands as one of the truly remarkable feats in all of sports.

Navratilova's great contributions to the game of tennis are not limited to her fifty-five Grand Slam titles (the Grand Slam is made up of tennis's four major tournaments—the Australian Open, the French Open, Wimbledon, and the U.S. Open), itself an astounding statistic. She also brought new levels of excitement and fan interest to women's tennis in the 1980s, adding speed, power, and strength to the game. She introduced new training methods, including strength training using weights, rigorous running regimens, and carefully monitored nutritional programs, all specifically designed for women tennis players.

Young Tennis Talent

Navratilova's journey to the top of the world of women's professional tennis began in her native Czechoslovakia at age four, when she got her first tennis racquet. At age six she took her first lesson. "The moment I stepped onto that crunchy red clay, felt the grit under my sneakers, felt the joy of smacking the ball over the net, I knew I was in the right place," she recalled.

When she was eight, Navratilova entered her first tournament. By the age of sixteen, she had become Czechoslovakia's top player. As her country's best tennis player, Navratilova was sent to the United States in 1973 to play in the eight-week U.S. Lawn Tennis Association's tournament circuit. It was during this tour that she played against Chris Evert for the first time. Navratilova lost, but the match marked the beginning of a

Chris Evert (right) and Navratilova, both consummate pros, shared a rivalry as well as a friendship for more than fifteen years.

fifteen-year rivalry. During that time, the two women would dominate and redefine the sport.

Dominating the Sport

In 1975, Navratilova defected to the United States. By the mid-1980s, she was well on her way to setting new standards for women's tennis, as she changed the look and style of the game. Navratilova won six Wimbledon titles in a row, from 1982 to 1987, bringing her total to eight. Then in 1990, she returned to the finals against Zina Garrison, a twenty-six-year-old from Houston. That year, Garrison became the first African-American woman to reach the Wimbledon finals since Althea Gibson won back-to-back championships in 1957 and 1958.

Determined to break Helen Wills Moody's record, Navratilova fought fiercely, dominating Garrison—who had defeated Monica Seles and Steffi Graf, two of the sport's top players,

Navratilova reacts with relief and joy after winning her eighth Wimbledon title in 1987.

NAVRATILOVA'S WIMBLEDON VICTORIES

Year	Opponent	Score
1990	Zina Garrison	6–4, 6–1
1987	Steffi Graf	7–5, 6–3
1986	Hana Mandlikova	7–6 (7–1), 6–3
1985	Chris Evert-Lloyd	4–6, 6–3, 6-2
1984	Chris Evert-Lloyd	7–6 (7–5), 6–2
1983	Andrea Jaeger	6–0, 6–3
1982	Chris Evert-Lloyd	6–1, 3–6, 6–2
1979	Chris Evert-Lloyd	6–4, 6–4
1978	Chris Evert	2–6, 6–4, 7–5

to reach the finals—by scores of 6–4 in the first set and 6–1 in the second. Navratilova froze Garrison with her serves and volleys. Lunging and spinning on her returns, she was a powerful blur of athletic grace.

Following her record-setting victory, Martina Navratilova dropped to her knees on the grass at Wimbledon, tears filling her eyes. Not only had she won her ninth championship, but the thirty-three-year-old champ in a sport dominated by youth became the oldest woman to win at Wimbledon in seventy-six years.

"I can't comprehend even one title," Garrison said afterward. "Nine is amazing. She really believes it's her court, and no one can take it away from her."

BATTLE OF THE SEXES

Billie Jean King, an outspoken advocate of equal rights for women, was one of the top tennis players of the 1960s and 1970s. During that period, she won 67 Women's Tennis Association singles titles, including 30 Grand Slam championships. King ranks fifth all-time with 695 total victories.

In the late 1960s and early 1970s, she led the fight to gain recognition for women's tennis, as the game was evolving from an amateur to a professional sport. Then, in 1973, fifty-five-year-old former tennis champion Bobby Riggs challenged King to a "battle of the sexes" to "prove" that tennis was a man's game.

On September 20 of that year they met in the Houston Astrodome, a baseball stadium, before the largest number of people ever to witness a tennis match—30,472 spectators at the Astrodome and another 50 million watching on TV.

In an incredibly powerful victory for the women's movement and for women's tennis, King whipped Riggs 6–4, 6–3, 6–3. Later King said, "This is the culmination of a lifetime in the sport. Tennis has always been reserved for the rich, the white, the males—and I've always been pledged to change all that."

Her victory in Houston was a large step on the road to achieving that change. Today, thanks in no small part to King's determination and willingness to engage in a match that was part sport, part theater, and part political activism, the women's game has become one of the biggest draws in all of professional sports.

BATTLE TO A SHOOT-OUT

The Final Game of the 1999 Women's World Cup

If this book were about only one great moment—the greatest moment—in the history of women's sports, it would have to be the final game of the Women's World Cup in 1999.

The enormous Rose Bowl—a college football stadium usually reserved for the all-male activity of NCAA football—was completely sold out. The largest crowd ever to witness a women's sporting event—90,185 people—packed the legendary

Mia Hamm brought both leadership and great ball-handling skills to the U.S. soccer team.

stadium. A few years earlier, this would have been inconceivable, but here it was, a women's sporting event drawing as many spectators, as large a television audience—40 million viewers, the largest audience for any soccer match in network TV history—as much pre-game media hype and post-game media coverage as any men's sporting event.

Twenty-seven years after Title IX, at least for a brief time, a women's sporting event was just as important as a men's competition. The equality of recognition—which women athletes had long craved and gotten a taste of when Babe Didrikson Zaharias shattered the world's expectations of what a woman could do as an athlete—had finally been achieved. The thrilling finish to the final game of the 1999 Women's World Cup was the culmination of a three-week, sixteen-team, thirty-two-match tournament.

Tenacious goalkeeper Briana Scurry held the Chinese scoreless during regulation play and then blocked one of China's penalty kicks during the shoot-out in overtime.

Crowd Favorites

Following their gold medal victory in the 1996 Olympics, the pressure was squarely on the shoulders of the U.S. women's soccer team. The players understood that going into the 1999 World Cup, with the United States as the host country, they were more than just athletes—they were also ambassadors for the sport during a tournament that had the eyes of the world focused on women's soccer.

Following a thrilling, come-from-behind 3–2 victory over Germany in the quarterfinals, the United States enjoyed a hard-fought 2–0 win over Brazil in the semifinals. Then the U.S. squad faced off against China—the team they had defeated for Olympic gold in 1996—for the World Cup, which was last won by the United States in 1991.

A tense U.S. team watches as Brandi Chastain takes the final penalty kick of the World Cup finals.

A Scoreless Tie

After battling in an epic struggle for ninety minutes of regulation play, neither team had scored. They next played two fifteen-minute sudden-death-overtime periods, but again, no goals were scored. This meant that penalty kicks would decide who would be champion.

China scored on four of its five penalty kicks. U.S. goaltender Briana Scurry had dived to block the third Chinese kick, which came from 12 yards (10.9 m) out. That feat would prove to be the biggest save of Scurry's career.

The United States made its first four kicks to tie the score. It was then up to Brandi Chastain to nail down the victory. Her kick sailed past the Chinese goaltender and into the net, sealing the win for the United States. Chastain dropped to her knees, pumped her fists in the air, and triumphantly tore off her outer uniform shirt, a gesture symbolic of the liberation of women's sports from years of second-class citizenry.

Role Models and Stars

In the days that followed their victory, the team became media stars, appearing on talk shows such as *The Late Show with David Letterman*, shooting a series of funny commercials with superstars such as Michael Jordan, and inspiring a generation of young girls to join youth-league soccer teams, which saw an incredible rise in participation, as girls around the country dreamed of becoming the next Brandi Chastain or Mia Hamm.

The seeds planted by Title IX had finally blossomed, and the effects of the 1999 Women's World Cup team on future generations are already being felt.

An exuberant Brandi Chastain falls to her knees after scoring the winning penalty kick against China.

THE ROAD TO THE ROSE BOWL

Here are the key moments in the quest for the 1999 Women's World Cup:

June 19: The third Women's World Cup opens at Giants Stadium in New Jersey, as 78,972 fans watch the United States shut out Denmark 3–0 on goals by Mia Hamm, Julie Foudy, and Kristine Lilly. That same day, China beats Sweden 2–1.

June 24: After giving up a goal just two minutes into the match, the U.S. team regains its composure and comes back to trounce Nigeria 7–1 in front of 65,080 fans at Soldier Field in Chicago.

June 26: China beats Australia 3–1 to complete an undefeated run in the first phase of World Cup competition. They have outscored their opponents 12–2 so far.

June 27: The U.S. team blanks North Korea 3–0 in Foxboro, Massachusetts, to advance to the quarterfinals.

July 1: In front of 54,642 fans—including President Bill Clinton and his family—in Landover, Maryland, the United States comes from behind to beat Germany 3–2 to advance to the semifinals. Tiffeny Millbrett, Brandi Chastain, and Joy Fawcett score the three U.S. goals.

July 4: The U.S. team defeats Brazil 2–0 in the semifinals, advancing to the finals against China, who beat Norway 5–0.

July 10: The U.S. team wins the Women's World Cup, beating China after ninety scoreless regulation minutes and two fifteen-minute sudden-death overtime periods, when Briana Scurry blocks a kick by China's Liu Ying and Brandi Chastain drills home the winning penalty kick.

SMASHING SIXTY

Annika Sorenstam Shoots a Fifty-nine

Golf is an extremely precise game, one that requires remarkable concentration. When driving, players not only have to focus on the flag, but they also have to take wind direction and speed into account. When putting, they have to ignore external distractions while analyzing the breaks on the green. Sometimes even a score of par—an average score for a particular course, usually in the range of 71 to 73—can seem impossible. A few small mis-

Annika Sorenstam approaches the green at the 2001 Standard Register PING tournament, where she shot a record 59.

takes can mean the difference between a double bogey (two over par on a given hole) and a birdie (one under par).

On March 16, 2001, in the second round of the 2001 Standard Register PING tournament in Phoenix, Arizona, golfer Annika Sorenstam did something spectacular. She didn't just break par. She didn't just score a handful of birdies for an above-average day. She scored a 59 on a round of golf, becoming only the fourth professional golfer and the first woman ever to do so.

Growing up with Golf

Sorenstam was born in Stockholm, growing up amid the Swedish tennis boom of the 1970s. By the time she was sixteen, however, she had burned out on tennis and so turned her legendary work ethic—she is known to spend endless hours practicing—to golf.

Painfully shy as a teenager, Sorenstam would deliberately miss putts to lose tournaments, since winning meant giving a victory speech afterward. After winning a local junior tournament, she spoke to the crowd for one minute and learned that it wasn't as bad as she had feared.

The young phenom first gained notice in 1991, winning the NCAA golf championship

In addition to scoring that record 59 in March 2001, Sorenstam has won a number of major tournaments including, shown here, the 1996 U.S. Women's Open.

while attending the University of Arizona. In 1994, she was the Ladies Professional Golf Association (LPGA) Tour's Rookie of the Year. By 1996, she had won several U.S. Women's Open titles and was quickly becoming recognized as the top woman golfer in the world.

In the Record Book

It was a sunny, windless day as the thirty-year-old lined up a long putt. She tapped her

THAT SECOND ROUND			
Hole	Yards	Par	Sorenstam's score
1	349 (319 m)	4	3 (birdie)
2	169 (154 m)	3	2 (birdie)
3	336 (307 m)	4	3 (birdie)
4	511 (467 m)	5	4 (birdie)
5	136 (124 m)	3	3 (par)
6	393 (359 m)	4	4 (par)
7	401 (367 m)	4	4 (par)
8	476 (435 m)	5	4 (birdie)
9	383 (350 m)	4	4 (par)
10	534 (488 m)	5	4 (birdie)
11	157 (143 m)	3	2 (birdie)
12	394 (360 m)	4	3 (birdie)
13	506 (462 m)	5	4 (birdie)
14	355 (324 m)	4	3 (birdie)
15	177 (162 m)	3	2 (birdie)
16	414 (378 m)	4	3 (birdie)
17	360 (329 m)	4	3 (birdie)
18	408 (373 m)	4	4 (par)
Totals		72	59 (13 under par)

Sorenstam lining up to sink a putt on her historic day.

putter on the ground, then paced off the 25 feet (7.63 m) to the hole. She strode to the opposite side of the green, crouched, and stared back at the hole. She returned to her ball and putted, then watched intently as the ball rolled to a stop 8 inches (20.32 centimeters) from the hole. Her tap-in for a birdie completed the record-shattering round. Annika Sorenstam leaped into her caddie's arms, then kissed her husband to celebrate her entry into the ranks of golf's all-time greats.

"Well, at first I was happy I made the putt because it felt like one of the longest putts I've had all day, even though it may not have been distance-wise," she explained. "After I sunk it, I was trying to count really quickly to see if I counted right at first, because I didn't want to just jump up and down when I thought I had shot a 59, when really it might have been a 60. Then I saw my caddie, and I said 'I did shoot 59, didn't I?' And he said 'Yeah, you did,' And so it was."

Sorenstam chips onto the green on that record-setting day in March 2001.

"It shows that we [women] can play," Sorenstam said afterward. "There's some good scoring out here, and I wish people could see that. I think girls out here do a good job."

What made Annika Sorenstam's round of 59 even more incredible was the fact that of the eighteen holes she played, thirteen were completed for birdies, and the rest for par. It is a feat that few others will ever accomplish.

"I don't try to be in the spotlight," Sorenstam says about the attention she has received. "I like my game to speak for itself." With one amazing record already in the book and a bright future ahead of her, that game is speaking to the rest of the golf world, in a voice loud and clear.

Women's Sports Time Line

1904 American Lida Howell wins three gold medals in archery, becoming the first woman to win three gold medals in one Olympic sport.

1926 Gertrude Ederle becomes the first woman to complete the 21-mile (33.8-km) swim across the English Channel, something only five men had previously done.

1932 Babe Didrikson Zaharias wins two gold medals and a silver medal at the Olympics, becoming the first athlete to win individual medals in running, throwing, and jumping events.

1936 Figure skater Sonja Henie wins her third consecutive Olympic gold medal, a feat that no other skater has accomplished.

1943 The All-American Girls Professional Baseball League begins play, becoming the first women's professional baseball league to succeed on a national level.

1948 Alice Coachman becomes the first African-American woman to win an Olympic gold medal with her win in the high jump.

1957 Althea Gibson becomes the first African-American woman to win the Wimbledon and U.S. Open tennis tournaments.

1960 Wilma Rudolph becomes the first American woman runner to win three gold medals at a single Olympics.

1972 The U.S. Congress passes Title IX of the Education Amendments, ending discrimination against girls and women in federally funded programs.

1974 Girls play Little League Baseball for the first time.

1976 Romanian Nadia Comaneci receives the first perfect 10 score in the history of Olympic gymnastics.

1984 Joan Benoit Samuelson takes gold in the first-ever women's Olympic Marathon.

1988 Steffi Graf wins pro tennis's four major tournaments to capture a Grand Slam and takes the gold medal at the Olympic Games. Jackie Joyner-Kersee wins two Olympic gold medals, setting the still-standing world record in the heptathlon.

1990 Martina Navratilova wins a record ninth Wimbledon title.

1997 The Women's National Basketball Association (WNBA) begins play.

1998 Ila Borders of the Duluth-Superior Dukes, a minor-league baseball team, becomes the first woman to start a men's professional baseball game as a pitcher.

1999 The U.S. women's soccer team captures its second World Cup soccer title with a shoot-out victory over China.

2001 Annika Sorenstam becomes only the fourth professional golfer, and the first woman, to shoot a 59.

To Learn More

BOOKS

Hastings, Penny. *Sports for Her: A Reference Guide for Teenage Girls.* Westport, Conn.: Greenwood Publishing Group, 1999.

Longman, Jere. *The Girls of Summer: The U.S. Women's Soccer Team and How It Changed the World.* New York: HarperCollins, 2000.

Macy, Sue, and Jane Gottesman, editors. *Play Like a Girl: A Celebration of Women in Sports.* New York: Henry Holt, 1999.

Oglesby, Carole A., editor. *Encyclopedia of Women and Sport in America.* Phoenix: Oryx Press, 1998.

Ruth, Amy. *Wilma Rudolph.* Minneapolis: Lerner, 2000.

Steiner, Andy. *A Sporting Chance: Sports and Gender.* Minneapolis: Lerner, 1995.

Wakeman, Nancy. *Babe Didrikson Zaharias: Driven to Win.* Minneapolis: Lerner, 2000.

INTERNET SITES

Canadian Association for the Advancement of Women and Sport and Physical Activity
www.caaws.ca
A group that encourages women in all sports.

Sports Illustrated for Women
sportsillustrated.cnn.com/siwomen
For information about women athletes and current competitions.

Women's National Basketball Association
www.wnba.com
The official site of the WBNA.

Women's Sports Foundation
www.womenssportsfoundation.org
To learn more about women's roles in sports.

Women's United Soccer Association
www.wusa.com
For the latest news in women's soccer.

Index

ABOUT THE AUTHOR

Michael Teitelbaum has written and edited children's books and magazines for more than twenty years. He was editor of Little League Magazine for Kids, *is the author of a two-volume encyclopedia on the* Baseball Hall of Fame, *and is the writer/project editor of* Breaking Barriers: In Sports, In Life, *a character education program, which is based on the life of Jackie Robinson and was created for* Scholastic, Inc., *and Major League Baseball.*